Camping

Hunting and Fishing Books for Kids

By

Isiah Maxwell

© Copyright 2018
All rights reserved.

The content contained within this book may not be reproduced, duplicated or transmitted without direct written permission from the author or the publisher.

Under no circumstances will any blame or legal responsibility be held against the publisher, or author, for any damages, reparation, or monetary loss due to the information contained within this book. Either directly or indirectly.

Legal Notice:

This book is copyright protected. This book is only for personal use. You cannot amend, distribute, sell, use, quote or paraphrase any part, or the content within this book, without the consent of the author or publisher.

Disclaimer Notice:

Please note the information contained within this document is for educational and entertainment purposes only. All effort has been executed to present accurate, up to date, and reliable, complete information. No warranties of any kind are declared or implied. Readers acknowledge that the author is not engaging in the rendering of legal, financial, medical or professional advice. The content within this book has been derived from various sources. Please consult a licensed professional before attempting any techniques outlined in this book.

By reading this document, the reader agrees that under no circumstances is the author responsible for any losses, direct or indirect, which are incurred as a result of the use of information contained within this document, including, but not limited to, — errors, omissions, or inaccuracies.

Table Of Contents

Introduction 7

Chapter 1: Why Is Camping Fun? 8

    Reduces Distractions... 8

    Increases Your Problem-Solving Abilities 9

    Helps You to Battle Your Blues 10

    Gives You're the Chance To Discover New Places 11

    It Lets You Connect with Your Loved Ones 11

    Helps You to Learn and Hone Life-Skills............... 13

    Final Thoughts 13

Chapter 2: Equipment to Bring......................... 15

    Clothes.. 15

    Food and Drinks.. 16

    Sleeping Bag 17

    Flashlights 18

    Water Purifier.. 19

    First-Aid Kit 19

    Maps... 21

A Pack of Matches 22

Rope 22

Extra Clothes 23

A Small Spice Rack 23

Entertainment Essentials 24

Woolen Socks 25

Speakers 25

Face Wipes 25

Peanut Butter 26

Hammock 26

Chapter 3: Tips and Tricks 27

Matchbox Keeper 27

Toilet Paper Container 28

Beer-Can Popcorn 28

Use Your Frisbees Differently 29

Headlamp Lantern 29

Camping Pancakes 30

Pep Up Your Tour with Short Day/Night Trips ... 30

Packing Tips 32

Chapter 4: Safety Measures 33

Conduct Ample Research 33

Consider Medical Issues 34

Check Your Stove 37

Chapter 5: Keeping the Environment Clean 38

Dry Your Tent 38

Always Carry a Trash Can 39

Use Rugs and Tarps 40

Follow the Right Etiquette 40

Arrange For a Dishwashing Station 41

Screened Shelter Camps 42

Bring Camping Furniture 42

Use the Right Branches 43

Conclusion 44

Glossary 45

Isiah Maxwell

Introduction

Are you planning to go on a camping adventure? Do you want to make the most of your camping trip? If your answers are yes, then this book is exactly what you need to read! *Camping for Kids* is your definitive guideline to everything you've ever wanted to know about planning a camping trip.

Whether it's a checklist for the equipment, safety kits, or a list of tips and tricks to make your trip more exciting—this book covers it all. As you flip through the pages, you will find some innovative guidelines that are simple and incredibly easy to follow.

So read on for the best camping guidelines that will surely double the fun of your camping trip!

Chapter 1: Why Is Camping Fun?

Camping isn't just about packing your bags and heading out for an adventure; rather, it is an opportunity to set yourself loose, disconnect from your regular life, and witness every possible experience that life has in store for you.

But in spite of its innumerable advantages, many people think twice before camping, fearing the expenses or environmental hazards that might come along the way. Ironically, most of these fears are baseless because if you plan things the right way, nothing will be as exciting and enjoyable as camping. In case you're still skeptical, here are a couple of reasons why camping is fun!

Reduces Distractions

When you head out for a camping trip, you leave your television, video games, phone, and every other electronic gadget at home. Since these gadgets compel you to have lesser contact with the world around you, camping automatically cuts down on these distractions. As a part of your camping trip, you get an opportunity to hunt for treasures, take walks in a beautiful, picturesque rural setting, and sing songs by the campfire with your loved ones. All of this is much better than sitting at home, constantly playing video games.

Increases Your Problem-Solving Abilities

At times, camping and the activities associated with it bring forth tough and mind-boggling challenges. Most of these challenges are things that you haven't dealt with in your regular life. For instance, setting up your tent, keeping yourself calm in adverse weather conditions or cooking with friends aren't the things you do regularly. So when you go out for camping, you get to explore the new while also stepping out of your comfort zone. At the end of the day, this plays a vital role in building your problem-solving abilities.

Helps You to Battle Your Blues

One of the biggest reasons why you need to camp is because of the positive impact it has on your mood. According to an analysis conducted by the Center for Cultural Studies, camping has a major role in improving your overall well-being and mood. And it doesn't just stop there! In addition to making you feel happy and comfortable, it also reduces your burnout and helps you to handle your responsibilities better.

When you go for a camping trip, you end up unwinding, thereby accepting everything that comes along the way. So if you're an uptight person who has major issues in stepping out of your comfort zone, camping will help you to lighten up. As you camp, it is very likely that you'll be stuck in certain situations that you didn't expect at all. And it is these very situations that will help you to embrace the change and uncertainty that life burdens you with. If you want to move ahead in life, you will have to accept change—and when it comes to accepting change, there's no better teacher than the experiences you gain while camping.

Gives You're the Chance To Discover New Places

One of the defining aspects of camping is the fact that it helps you to discover new places. As you go for a camping tour, you get an opportunity to explore the wilderness like never before. It increases your experiences and also offers you an excellent opportunity to rediscover wilderness and forests in a new light.

It Lets You Connect with Your Loved Ones

There is an age-old notion that when you

frequently camp, you drift away from your family. But this notion is completely baseless. Contrarily, when you head out for a camping trip, you don't just establish newer connections but also strengthen your existing relationships. The idea behind this is pretty simple. When you camp with a group of people, it feels easier to meet and approach new people. This is primarily because you operate in an environment which is completely different from your daily routine. As you continue meeting people, you don't just build newer connections but also feel a sense of gratitude for the connections you already have in your life.

Similarly, when you camp with your family, it leaves a great impact on your existing relationships with them. Camping gives you a chance to relax which eventually plays a part in increasing your relationship's satisfaction. On top of that, as you participate in more activities with your family and loved ones, it creates a lasting sense of connection. You cherish your relationships, get to spend more time with the people who really matter, and also get an opportunity to build memories and stories that'll be cherished for years down the line.

Helps You to Learn and Hone Life-Skills

When you take your kids out for a camping trip, you get a chance to teach them valuable life-lessons. For instance, you get to teach them the art of making a campfire, gathering wood, and cooking over open coals. You also get a chance to teach them about hunting small animals, tracking in the woods, finding directions without a compass, and so on. Kids enjoy these small activities and the overall experience turns out to be wholesome and enjoyable.

Final Thoughts

Camping is a once-in-a-lifetime experience. After

all, there are very few activities that are more enjoyable than sitting by a campfire and sharing heartfelt stories. Camping gives you the chance to reflect upon your life differently. It also helps you to connect with your buddies, share stories with them, and try new, interactive activities with them. Kids who go camping with their parents get to connect with adults in a new, unique way. They understand their parents better and also get a chance to spend some quality time with them. So, if you still have second thoughts about camping, think no more, and head out for your camping adventure right away!

Chapter 2: Equipment to Bring

Your camping trip is incomplete without the right equipment. Although an extensive stay amid the wilderness doesn't require much clothing or shoes, there are always a couple of essentials that you can't leave out. In this chapter, we will discuss these essentials that will make your camping trips even more enjoyable.

Clothes

When you are packing for a camping trip, every single piece of equipment will count. So, when you're choosing clothes, try to pick lightweight fabrics that have moisture-wicking properties. In this way, you will get a chance to reuse your same shirt and pants a couple of times. In addition to these clothes, you should also include lightweight hats, waterproof jackets, woolen socks, boots (for hiking), and sunglasses. While choosing sunglasses, opt for polarized shades as they block the bright sunrays from affecting your face.

You should also carry a pair of long pants and long-sleeved shirts. Add these to your list even when the forecast seems to be warm, as the nights might be cool. Finally, pick some water-shoes, sandals, and a compression cube set. This set will help you in organizing all the items.

Food and Drinks

Since camping calls for cooking your own meals, it is also important to carry the right cooking equipment. In case you're wondering what to carry, here's a quick list:

- Camping stove – You need to carry a portable camping stove that is not just easy to carry, but is equally convenient to set up. While carrying this stove, also carry adequate fuel.

- Cooking utensils – Carry utensils for both

cooking and eating.

- Small, portable water bottles
- Cutting board
- Snacks – Although you'll be whipping up your own meals during the trip, it is really important to carry a couple of pre-packaged snacks. Try to include plenty of bars, trail mixes, and freeze-dried camping meals in your backpack.
- A good knife
- Electric kettle

Sleeping Bag

Also known as camping blankets, sleeping bags keep you warm as you're sleeping by the forest. These bags also cushion your body and keep you a little more comfortable. While some campers also recommend sleeping pads, it isn't really necessary for first-timers.

You can also carry a tent or a bivy-style bag if you're planning to experience the extremes. Both the tent and the bivy bag will keep you safe from extreme weather conditions. We would suggest you choose bivy-bags over conventional tents because they take up less space and are much more comfortable than your regular tent.

Flashlights

Your camping trip is absolutely incomplete without the right set of flashlights. These lights are not only important for your safety, but they also help you to maintain your sanity amid the wilderness. When it comes to choosing a flashlight, opt for a small, lightweight variant that comes with an easy-to-activate switch. In addition to this, also make sure that the flashlight comfortably fits in your hand and pumps up lots of lumens.

Although some campers choose headlamps over flashlights, we would suggest you carry both for better safety.

Water Purifier

Regardless of the destination, you should never drink water from ponds or lakes while camping since even the purest of stream water carries a wide range of lethal pathogens. To put it simply—a single sip from an abandoned creek can ruin your entire trip and cause you to head to the emergency room.

Now, while there are several ways to purify water, most campers opt for water purifiers as they are both convenient and effective. We suggest you bring one purifier for every two individuals in your group. This will ensure that you get clear streams of water as quickly as you want.

First-Aid Kit

Although certain campers will choose a couple of basic first-aid utilities in their survival kit, every camping trip should come with a perfectly stocked first-aid kit. In case you're wondering what to include in this kit, here's a short list:

- 10-15 bandages
- Tape and gauze
- A pair of tweezers
- Benadryl and aspirin
- Ibuprofen and any pain-relieving lotions
- Medication for diarrhea
- Antacid or any other medication for indigestion
- Antiseptic wipes
- Moleskin
- Antibiotic ointment

In addition to this, you should also bring every other prescription medication that you might need during the trip. Also make sure that the first-aid items are well-packed in a solid carrying case. In this way, all the items are perfectly organized.

You should also choose a brightly colored bag for the first-aid kit since it'll be easier to locate during an emergency.

Maps

If you want to reach your intended destination on the trip, you will need a good map for getting there. This map is incredibly useful when you're hiking marked trails as it allows you to check the distance you've traveled and the distance that you need to travel to reach your camping spot.

You can also opt for digital maps that are available on your phone or tablets. These maps are easily available and they provide immense value during an emergency. However, despite carrying a digital map, we recommend you carry paper maps as the former usually depends on good cell phone signals.

A Pack of Matches

Unless you're an experienced Boy Scout, you'll need some kind of flame for starting a fire. And if you don't have a fire, your food options will be limited and nights will be chillier. So instead of taking any risks, buy plenty of matches in advance. Once you have them, you can always leave these matches in your bag of camping essentials.

Rope

Ropes have plenty of uses around a campsite, particularly if you're smart enough to tie several knots at once. You can use a rope for making a clothing line for wet garments, hanging your food bag from a branch, creating a shelter, or towing people out of tight situations.

Extra Clothes

Even if you've checked the weather forecast several weeks before your trip, it is important to carry an extra pair of clothes, an umbrella and a raincoat for adverse weather conditions. The weather can always change all of a sudden, leaving you in the middle of rain and thunderstorms. So when you have an extra pair of clothes and a raincoat, you can swap your wet clothes for the fresh ones and stay safe and dry even in the coldest fronts.

A Small Spice Rack

Since nobody loves under-seasoned meals, it is always a good idea to carry a small portable spice rack at your campsite. This rack will perfectly hold your spices while also adding an extra zing to your meals.

Entertainment Essentials

One of the coolest things about a camping trip is spending some good time with your friends and loved ones, without any common distractions of our urban life. But avoiding distractions doesn't mean you can't carry some entertainment essentials. You can always carry a binocular, a hood camera, board games, cards, fishing gear (like reels and poles), kayaking equipment and bikes to double the fun of your trip.

In case you're planning to hike for the majority of the days, leave out the board games and carry more hiking essentials. Alternatively, you're going for a school trip that involves more interactive activities and less hiking, carry plenty of games, cards and activity books.

Heading for a camping trip is your opportunity to push your boundaries and experience new things. So, chat with your friends, read and share inspirational camping stories to make the most out of your trip.

Woolen Socks

While this might come as a surprise to many, woolen socks are a great item as they offer maximum comfort. These socks are all the more necessary if you plan on hiking, as the soft wool will keep your feet warm during your trail.

Speakers

If you're camping with your buddies, playing good music is an excellent way to set the right mood. You can always play some music after you head back from a hiking trip to your tent. The music will charge you and maximize your fun throughout the trip.

Face Wipes

When you're camping in the wilderness, you'll have limited access to water. In this situation, you wouldn't want to use this water by washing your face. So as an alternative option, it is always a great idea to carry a couple of face wipes and moisturizers to stay perfectly fresh throughout the day.

Peanut Butter

Peanut butter comes with a long shelf life, and you can use it in several ways than you would usually imagine. As an excellent source of protein and fat, you should carry this for every camping trip. Peanut butter can be smeared on your bread, used for removing gum from your hair and be eaten at night while you're enjoying by your campfire.

Hammock

There's no better feeling than resting by your hammock under a huge, shady tree at the end of a tedious hike. Since hammocks are small, lightweight and portable they won't take up much space in your bag.

Chapter 3: Tips and Tricks

Camping is fun. But what if you could make it all the more exciting? Yes, you can add a dash of fun to your camping trip by following a couple of simple tips and tricks. In the next section, you will find detailed insight on these tips.

Matchbox Keeper

While camping is definitely fun, it does come with its fair share of weather issues. Even when you check the forecast, it is impossible to predict whether it'll rain or not. And this is exactly why you need a special matchbox keeper that'll keep your matchsticks dry, regardless of the weather. You can easily create this by tracing a small circle on sandpaper at the center of your mason jar's lid. Now add hot glue to attach the sandpaper circle to the circle on your mason jar. You can then easily store your matchsticks inside it.

Camping for Kids

Toilet Paper Container

You can keep your toilet paper safe and dry by using a plastic coffee jar as your toilet paper holder. Simply place the toilet paper inside and create a slit along the sides. This slit should be big enough for the paper to be pulled out. Now poke a small hole along the bottom of the can and run a string for hanging this toilet paper off the ground.

Beer-Can Popcorn

Add some popcorn kernels to an empty beer can and fill up one-fourth of it. Right after this, gently add some popcorn oil and place the beer can along the edge of your campfire. Now wait till your kernels pop. Once the popping slows down a little, remove the can, cut it in half, and enjoy your beer-can popcorn.

Use Your Frisbees Differently

Frisbees aren't just for playing or throwing around. If used the right way, they can be your plates, cutting board, bowls, or even a mortar. If you clean them well, you can also use them to collect rainwater or as replacement paddles while you're kayaking around.

Headlamp Lantern

If you need the light from a lantern but only have access to a small headlamp, you can always convert it into a makeshift lantern. The idea is simple; take a gallon milk jug, or a detergent container, and clean it properly. After this, attach your headlamp with the light facing the interior of the jug to expand the glow of your headlamp lantern.

Camping Pancakes

You can easily save the hassle of preparing pancakes at the campsite by bringing your pre-made pancake mix from home. You can then store this mix in a disposable frosting bag that is tied along the end. When you plan to cook, all you have to do is snip its end for creating a top that will dispense the batter. Once you're done with the mix, throw the bags away or clean them out for reuse.

Pep Up Your Tour with Short Day/Night Trips

It goes without saying that this is one of the very first things that you need to do while camping. Your trip will incomplete if you don't spend enough time touring the city, strolling the streets, and visiting the nearby cultural hubs. You can start off by making a list of the best places in your chosen destination. Once you have it ready, head out with your Google map and visit every single spot that defines the city/town you're traveling in. If you want to be a little more adventurous, ditch your map and ask the locals about nearby spots. This will not just help you with navigation but will play an equally important role in helping you establish newer connections.

As you head out, try visiting the picturesque beaches, the lofty mountains, the spectacular art galleries/museums, the quaint restaurants, and every other place that has been recommended to you. Every town/city has a unique set of activities as well. This can be anything ranging from trekking, kayaking, paragliding, street hopping, wine tasting, or virtually anything under the sun. So, if you're an adventurous person, participate in these activities to make the most out of your time. Once you manage to use your leisure time to its full potential, you'll be left with thousands of unforgettable experiences that'll surely leave a positive impact on your life.

Packing Tips

Packing for your camping tour might seem easy, but things can get quite messy if you don't have the right plan at hand. In following section we've listed some tips, that'll make it easier for you to pack everything you need-

- Keep a small list of the things you'll need for the trip, and check if they are easily available.

- Start packing your bags at least fourteen days before your trip. Last minute bag packing will give you nothing but stress,

- Always check a 10-day weather forecast.

- While packing your bags, put your most necessary items after putting everything else. In this way, these items will be easily accessible.

- Use cargo carriers to avoid space crunch.

Chapter 4: Safety Measures

While camping can be fun and exciting, it is also equally important to ensure proper safety during your camping trips. In this chapter, we will discuss the safety measures that you should follow.

Conduct Ample Research

Even before you plan your trip, it is really important to conduct some relevant research. Read about your destination in detail and find out whether you'll be near a forest, a beach, or a desert. Check the weather and find out whether you need to take precautions against mosquitoes, ticks, or dangerous snakes.

It is really important to learn about your destination because it helps you to stay prepared for the experiences that will come along your way. If you're planning to camp in a remote area, also take suggestions from park rangers about the precautions you should be taking. This will keep you aware of the regulations pertaining to building fires, dangerous wildlife, options for food storage, and so on.

Consider Medical Issues

While preparing for your camping trip, it is also important to consider the health issues of the various members in your small (or big) group. In the following section, you will find some details about the considerations you need to take.

Organize your prescriptions – Like any other trip, it is really important to sort out your prescriptions and take them on your trip. This will help you if you suddenly misplace a certain medicine.

Make a list – In addition to organizing your prescriptions, you will also need to come up with a list of the medications, allergies, or contact details for every individual going on the trip. This information will help you in the instance of an accident.

Vaccination – Before you plan a camping trip, double-check whether you have the proper vaccinations. You should also check the current status of your tetanus and allergy shots.

Always Wear Bug Spray

When you're out camping with your friends, you won't really know what dangers might come your way. And this is exactly why you need to wear bug spray throughout your trip. Using bug spray is much more convenient than slapping mosquitos and it'll also keep you protected throughout the entire night.

Stay Hydrated

When you head out for a camping trip, chances are you'll run around in the hot sun throughout a large part of the day. So, in a situation like this, it's always wise to stay hydrated. Carry a water bottle throughout the trip and make it a point to drink eight glasses of water every day.

Water Safety

If your camping trip includes swimming and other similar activities, it is really important to ensure that your family abides by common water-safety measures. Using floatation devices for kids is one of the most important safety guidelines in this case. However, there are also a couple of other tips that you should follow:

- Follow all instructions and research about nearby lakes and pools. If you plan on boating, check the speed limits; if you're kayaking, look out for currents and deep underwater areas.

- Always check the weather before you head out for water sports. If it's raining, avoid water sports completely.

- Follow a feet-first method of entry if the water is extremely shallow.

- If you are an adult, do not drink alcohol while boating with your kid. This can put everyone in an adverse situation.

Check Your Stove

While an extra stove can always be useful during a camping trip, it also comes with dangerous possibilities. Therefore, in order to avoid any issues, never leave your stove unattended while the propane is still on. To add to this, you should also follow the directions from the manufacturer if you are using the stove for the first time.

You should only run the propane when you plan on lighting the burner. Make sure the ignition dial is set on low. This will help you to avoid fireballs and potential burns. You should also keep your body away from the stove while igniting it. In order to do this, you will have to use the igniter switch of the stove whenever you can. This is relatively safer than lighting a stove with matches or a lighter.

Chapter 5: Keeping the Environment Clean

While camping is definitely an adventurous occasion, it also requires you to maintain your basic responsibilities. And the first among these responsibilities is keeping the environment around you clean. Camping in a clean environment won't just keep you safe, but it'll also double the fun of your trip. In this chapter, you will find some detailed guidelines on keeping your environment clean.

Dry Your Tent

If it has been raining along the site you're camping, always try to set your tent up afterwards. This will ensure that the tent completely dries out. In case you find small moldy areas, start off by brushing them off and cleaning them with a homemade solution.

You can add a cup of lemon juice and salt to a gallon of warm water for creating this solution. Once you have this ready, use it to clean your tent and other gear. Finally, let it dry for a while. After the gear and tent dry up, both of them will be free from unpleasant odors. If the process doesn't work the first instance, try it once again.

Always Carry a Trash Can

Camping calls for plenty of mess and this is exactly why you need to carry a small, portable trash can. Keep this trash can near your tent and dispose of all waste in it. Whether its snack wrappers or empty water bottles, make sure you dispose of them properly in your trash can. You can also use a trash bag, in case you don't have a small, portable trash can. This will keep your surroundings clean, and you'll no longer be invaded by frequent pests. Using a trash can also make it simpler to manage your unnecessary waste.

Use Rugs and Tarps

In addition to keeping the outdoors clean, you also want your tent environment to be comfortable. And one of the best ways to do this is by preventing it from getting messy right from the beginning. Experienced camping enthusiasts know to lay down an old tarp on which they set the tent. When the tent is up, they add another, newer tarp as a small buffer between their feet and the floor of the tent.

Alternatively, you can also use a woven rug right outside the flap of your tent. Almost every visitor will wipe their feet before they enter. This will also prevent dirt and mud from reaching the spots where you sleep.

Follow the Right Etiquette

When you do your final cleanup, it is really important to follow the right etiquette. To put it simply, you should scatter the rocks that you used for making your campfire ring, cover the latrines, pick up the pet droppings that you missed, and so on. Although this requires extra effort, it will help you to leave your campsite with a completely clear conscience and a stronger sense of accomplishment.

Arrange For a Dishwashing Station

If you are planning for a family camping trip, one of the biggest challenges you're likely to encounter is maintaining dishes. If you don't want to use paper plates and need proper dishes for the meals you have planned, try to bring three big tubs and some dishwashing soap. After you wake up in the morning, set these tubs up, fill them up with water, and take turns cleaning the dishes. Avoiding paper plates keeps your environment clean and using this simple strategy will make dishwashing easier.

P.S. While packing the soap, ensure that it is

biodegradable.

Screened Shelter Camps

If you've planned a camping trip in a screened shelter, try to carry a mop, a couple of buckets, a small hose, and a broom on your trip. You can then mop the concrete floor of the shelter by using a solution of bleach water. Once you're done with that, you can easily hose down the interiors of the shelter. While it does take a little more time for unpacking, it will comfortably sanitize the floor and prevent spiders from reaching your tent.

Bring Camping Furniture

Camping furniture is an excellent way to cut down on the environmental impact and stay more comfortable. So, when you bring camp chairs, for instance, you will no longer be tempted to move rocks for seats. In this way, you will get to camp comfortably without affecting the natural habitat.

Use the Right Branches

A camping trip is incomplete without a good campfire. However, while building the campfire, make sure you only do it in established rings where you can use dead and downed wood. This wood shouldn't be bigger than your forearm. If the situation permits, you can also buy firewood from a local station. Do not, under any circumstance, burn your trash. Burn all the used-up branches to ash and put your fire completely out before leaving.

Conclusion

Now that you've reached the end of this book, it is likely that you know everything that you wanted to know about camping. So, follow these guidelines, maintain proper safety measures, and only then will you be able to make the most of your camping trip. Happy camping!

Glossary

Environmental hazard – An item or situation that can cause harm to the environment.

Wilderness – Forested areas

Makeshift – Temporary

Picturesque – Spectacular

Tarp – A sheet cover for tarpaulin

Biodegradable – A substance that can be decomposed by bacteria

Manufactured by Amazon.ca
Bolton, ON